Small Comforts

Small Comforts

Poems by

LaDeana Mullinix

© 2025 LaDeana Mullinix. All rights reserved.
This material may not be reproduced in any form, published,
reprinted, recorded, performed, broadcast,
rewritten, or redistributed without
the explicit permission of LaDeana Mullinix.
All such actions are strictly prohibited by law.

Cover design by Shay Culligan
Cover image by Njeromin on Pexels

ISBN: 978-1-63980-679-9
Library of Congress Control Number: 2024953006

Kelsay Books
502 South 1040 East, A-119
American Fork, Utah 84003
Kelsaybooks.com

To all who have inspired and encouraged me.

Acknowledgments

I would like to express my gratitude to the editors of the following journals in which my poems have appeared, some in slightly altered form:

Friends Journal: "Tutoring James," "To the Women Who Attend Quaker Worship at the Fayetteville Women's Correctional Facility"
Medicine and Meaning: "40° Out of 180," "and the other's gold," "Elegy for Eight Words," "Philip," "Something New"
Midwest Quarterly: "Impossible Dreams"
Midwest Review: "Cellar of the Heart"
Slant: A Journal of Poetry: "Sumo's Tree," "Worth the Whuppin'," "For Chou," "Rose-Colored"

"Sonnenizio for Marianne" won the Betty Heildelberger Memorial Award of the Poets Roundtable of Arkansas
"Legacy of Birds" was short-listed for the Arthur Smith Poetry Prize in 2023

Contents

Sailing the Great Plains	13
Along New Highway 81	15
Why I Plant Flowers on a Stranger's Grave	16
Finding Brenda Gail	17
Impossible Dreams	19
Worth the Whuppin'	21
Peaches and Sin	23
The Painted Prayer at Les Ezies de Tayac	24
To the Women Who Attend Quaker Worship at the	25
Fayetteville Women's Correctional Facility	25
Autumn Daffodils	27
To a Sunflower Growing in the House	28
Sonnenizio for Marianne	29
Rising	30
Missionaries	31
Sumo's Tree	33
Philip	34
Lovey and the Queen	36
Dead Horse	37
Reincarnation of Little Chief	38
For Chou	40
"and the other's gold"	41
Something New	42
Small Comforts	44
Elegy for Eight Words	47
40° Out of 180—Song of the Scapula	48
Ode to Estivation	50
For My Young Friend Afraid He Learns Too	51
Slowly	51
Tutoring James	52
Slightly Up	53
Gym Friends	55

The Domino Effect	56
Rose-Colored	57
Learning to Pray in French	58
Cellar of the Heart	60

Sailing the Great Plains

In formation like the Pinta, the Niña,
and the Santa Maria,
the old hay wagons were docked
in the south pasture
against a row of hedge apple.

When new, they were pulled
by a team of Clydesdales
whose feathery fetlocks tricked many
to think their light steps were not powerful.

Young Quaker brothers
in white shirts,
black pants, black hats,
pitched unbaled hay
smelling of Heaven
onto wagons,
then into the loft
with an effort hidden
by its grace.

In retirement,
the wagons
took on late life careers
as pirate ships,
Conestoga wagons,
a safari caravan.

I favored Maria,
as her mast was the tallest,
her foot-snagging holes the fewest.
Her one-axle voice grated
with operatic volume
as I ran from bow to stern
and back—a one-girl teeter-totter.

In Kansas, you can see forever—
at least to a ship falling
over the green horizon.

On the Santa Maria
I could explore the past
I'd only glimpsed,
and create my new world.

Along New Highway 81

In my view west, driving north,
some Yorkshire pigs stood
on the second floor looking south.
No walls blocked their sight.
They could look east
with a slight turn of their eyes.

In another century,
blond children slept here
while their mama made biscuits,
holding her round cutter
by its red wooden handle.

In another world,
Pawnee youth with long legs
ran each year through auburn prairie grass
here to the southwest
on their spring adventure.

In another generation,
any memory of the vanishing Kansas farmhouse
will be wind-blown, weathered as
the red handle in black dirt.

But in that moment,
just north of Concordia,
those pigs looked happy.

Why I Plant Flowers on a Stranger's Grave

No other but her little grave bears
their surname:
"Our baby Adeline 1911."

Were they traveling?
Down on their luck?
Abandoning a dream?

Mama's Aunt Mamie lost their toddler
two years before they lost the farm.
Kansas dustbowl winds blew
their good black soil east
and they fled west where
Uncle finally found work
building the Grand Coulee Dam.

Please,
she said, *would you
sometimes
put a flower on his grave
so I'll know
he's not been forgotten?
The worst was leaving him
behind.*

So, Baby Adeline, the flowers
are for you, and for young Kansan Clare,
and for all children who left before it was fair,
and who were left behind
because life isn't.

Finding Brenda Gail

I can still spell Potawatomi and your name
Mzhickteno without hesitation.

Until it forked, the path of our youth
ran through the green Flint Hills, and
we were blown along it
by the ceaseless wind of the Great Plains.

We attended the same girls' "music class"
where we watched the film, then hid
(from the boys) our puberty pamphlets
in our songbooks.

With your family, I swayed in the summer night wind
at pow-wows, and the eternal pulse of the drums,
like a heartbeat, was blown just behind my breath,
where it lives today.

We discovered the Beatles together,
holding hands on my bedroom floor
and sighing significantly
whenever they inhaled
on our scratched little 45s.

We stood outside Woolworth's
and hollered, "We're horny!"
without knowing what
that word meant.

Together we learned the depth
of the word *half-mast*
that November day
at noon.

The letter to your brothers sits addressed,
but unwritten, for three weeks—

What do I say?

That, in searching for you,
I found instead
your obituary?

I'm sorry you died
before I could say some things.

I am sorry if kids
war-hooped at the boys
or called you squaw
on the school bus

and your anger,
fueled by frequency—
did it smolder?

I wish your mom
could know how
my life is spiced—
strong and sweet
as braided sweetgrass—

by the Potawatomi prairie
and the poignant inhalations
of Paul McCartney.

Impossible Dreams

I was two and TV was new
when I met Annette
the Mouseketeer.

When I was three, it was clear to me
Annette was aging, needed to be
replaced, so I learned her songs, dances,
and was free, ready for the call.

At four, Annette was out my door
and I flew with Peter Pan.
We threw two cans of chow
to any hungry dog.

By six, my reverie was to be
an ice skater—to stun and impress in my short little dress,
ready to twirl and leap at any sleepover,
recess, or school to-do.

When eight, my gate had opened wider
and I wanted to have been the writer
who penned *My Fair Lady,*
gracefully bowing to accolades.

One might want to say my young dreams,
solid and good, became the firm ground
on which my maturity stood.

But each dream had a ruinous fault:

Walt couldn't see Kansas from his studio,
didn't know I was good to go.

Hungry dogs couldn't open a can
and Tinker Bell swiped my man's affection.
While wearing ice skates clamped on with a key,
my problem was always going to be:
I can't skate.

My Fair Lady had a copyright.

Rather, my dreams gathered to weave a trampoline
with stripes, rickrack, and polka dots,
on which, even with my balance shot,
I can still bounce to the clouds and shout,
My God, that was fun!

Worth the Whuppin'

In the South in the summer,
brush hog is both what you have to do,
and what you have to do it with.

Just last week I heard
that our brush hog man Joe
once peed in his boss's gas can
to stretch out the fuel.

Do NOT tell him I told you,
said my source, so I will not.

Nor will I tell Joe I'm telling his tale
of Tom our neighbor—a yarn involving youth,
a pretty waitress, some roadkill
slapped on the counter, and too much beer.

But I *can* share the story told by a gentleman—a veteran
of the first Great War, living at the old City Hospital:
A covered dish social at church
on a warm June night before the war,
before TVs or telephones or model T's—
after supper, the parents tucked the tiny ones
into quilts in the wagons, the babies lulled to sleep
by the stomping of horses' hooves,
the jingling of harnesses.

The big boys then switched the children
so the Sanfords took home the Villines' boy
and their little girl went to the Young's.
The Whitley baby went to the Werner's warm kitchen,
while theirs went—well, you get the picture . . .
We got a whuppin', of course, he said,
but it was worth it
to hear the hollering.

These are not some preachy plots
of stuffy classics, nor parables from the Bible—

just little stories to say
we grew up OK—mostly—
and lived to swell the tale.

Peaches and Sin

So how was I to know that peach in French
is said the same as sin? When Soeur Marie
asked me, "But what of sin?" she gasped and clenched
her teeth when I replied with glee, *Ah, oui!*

Now peaches I like—*C'est bon! J'adore.* I thought
that she'd grown tired, like me, converting this
American, and moved to food. But her shocked,
huge eyes confirmed her feared analysis: a Protestant!
Well, hell (I'm sorry—heck)—
I'd only been in France a week, and sin
was not within my hundred-phrase cassette.
My soul would need her finest discipline.

Yes, I was saved by her—it's only fair
that praise be raised to her *dictionnaire.*

The Painted Prayer at Les Ezies de Tayac

(These prehistoric cave paintings are the only originals allowing visitors.)

Her models did not sit still on a stool for hours,
but ran to blend in the blowing wind,
camouflaging death.

She had no myriad hues in oil, pencil, acrylic,
but three colors: red, brown, black,
from clay, dirt, charcoal.

Did she (and why not she?) use her monthly periods
of banishment made bliss,
to paint her prayer on the grotto wall?

For thirty thousand years, her three colors have
beseeched these beasts, and blessed them,
nudged them to move by the thin light
slanting in under the overhang.

Their life, the first beautiful painted thing,
still runs with grace and gratitude.

To the Women Who Attend Quaker Worship at the Fayetteville Women's Correctional Facility

Were I a tree, I'd be,
with my luck, an oak—and
one with shriveled dry leaves
that cling all winter—

not glorious gold aspen
or radiant red maple leaves,
but the ones going from green
to brown in one cold, wet

October day, causing color seekers
to sigh and say: "Well, it was a
disappointing year." And with branches breaking
sometimes under the stress of ice or snow,

and the withered leaves hanging on
clear through early April,
an unwanted reminder of
grim winter amidst the splendor
of redbuds, dogwood,
and the springly green of
any worthy tree.

Ladies, for whatever reason
you sit in awkward holy silence
with us Quakers,
I want to tell you this:

The Force pushing off the old leaves
is strong, unstoppable, and coaxes out bold,
bright green leaves, forcing the dead ones
to the composting earth—

any sadness forgotten in the welcome summer shade.

Autumn Daffodils

Oh, they've wilted.
Pushing Miss Thelma
back to her room,
Shall I get you some fresh?

No.
She touches them gently
with twisted fingers—
They're still lovely.

To a Sunflower Growing in the House

Meant for the belly of a bird,
you somehow flew past the feeder top
and began, a seed nestled
in a Hawaiian ti flower pot,
to grow to window height,
facing a snow-covered deck
where juncos picked at seeds,
leaning your small golden petals
on the screen to prop you up.

Do you regret not being
in the garden among birds,
feeding them in fall as they perch
on your plate-size serving of seed,

or are you grateful to live
a stunted, unintended little longer,
and instead,
offer them a loveliness
rarely seen in February?

Sonnenizio for Marianne

When I consider how my light is spent,
I do not cradle the concern lightly.

All light is bestowed upon each
without effort, alights like a blessing—
a delightful commodity, unlimited,
unlike oil or the blight of coal.

We ought not squander the light we dispense,
but lighten the weight of sadness if we can,
allow joy to alight on a heavy world.

In Quaker parlance, to be *held in the Light*
is to be infused with prayer—a lightning strike of love,
a skylight to illuminate our way

so we can walk more lightly on the earth—
enlightened, to give our hope its worth.

(Kim Addonizio invented this form of the sonnet, calling it a sonnenizio. What you do is take a line—any line—from someone else's sonnet and use it as the first line of your sonnenizio. You then repeat one word from that first line in each of the subsequent 13 lines. You end the poem with a rhyming couplet.)

Rising

Green was gone, erased by ice.
Red of flower or feather—dead or flown.
Brown tarried on barren trees.

Gray asphalt
and the clouds lurking above—
gray as my heart, holding
the steely burden of guilt
to see my kind
cover and smother
our earth with hardness.

From beneath, a rising,
resounding, resting in my soul.
I felt more
than heard Her call

I'm still here,
waiting for the walking to wake,
gasping through cracks in cement.

Missionaries

That it was
April made
the sleet
more cruel.
Five dark days
hid the sun.
Arrows of ice
shot again into
my warm neck,
melting to a pool
just there
above my collarbone,
drowning all hope
that spring
would come.

But then
to lead us
came the ducks.

As we bent,
they opened beaks
on extended necks—
some spread wings,
duck tails wagging,
quacking their delight:

O blessed day!
It's STILL raining!
Rain, lovely rain
O duck luck!

Listening, I laughed,
baptized with joy,
stepping strong with
that fervor of

the newly converted.

Sumo's Tree

We buried your still-warm body
under your favorite tree—a ginko—
the first one you climbed
as a kitten, with the pride
of a panther
without the prowess.

Last year,
astounded by your
first falling leaves,
you chased that flying herd
of golden gazelles.

This year,
the leaves fell
far too early and blanketed
your fresh grave in green.

Next year,
the part of you
that was will become
part of your tree.
The part of you that
still is
already is.

Philip

We named you posthumously
since you died the same day
as the prince—April 9, 2021.
You had much in common—

old, loved, regally tall, and we knew
you were failing,
losing some substance up top.
Still, we were not ready,

and you'd think we might have heard
a two-story black gum fall
in the night.
But thunder covered your collapse,

and there you were,
dead on the damp earth in the morning
as we walked the dog,
lifting him over your fresh corpse.

Luckily the moon, though waning,
had wooed you to the east
so you didn't
crush us, sleeping 15 feet away,

nor the little white dog.
We left you to rest—too heavy to roll,
remaining a testament
to gentility, aristocracy among trees.

It will be a year next month—
warm enough to sit
on the bench you've become,
and have a cup of tea.

Lovey and the Queen

We were quite close but
she never knew.
She became queen the year I was born,
was always my friend.

I could've been her friend—
a good friend—
in another realm.

I befriended Lovey
after old neighbor Mary died
and left her old cat outside,
which Lovey liked.
She refused to leave Mary's yard.

For a year I fed, held, brushed her daily,
warmed her water in winter—
Royal attention.

Lovey died a week before the queen.

I wonder how long a soul waits
(a month, a millennium?)
communing with a prince, a papa, prime ministers
or with Tucker the tabby tom next door,

before choosing to carry on
and move along to a new life,
maybe switching to try an untraveled path

as an eminent aristocrat
or a loyal little green-eyed cat.

Dead Horse

On her side, unburied, still, and bloated—
human cruelty, I think,
to let her rot and reek so
with her partner close by.

Next day, dead bloated horse
not dead, but thin horse
nuzzling and nursing
wobbly long-legged foal.

Reincarnation of Little Chief

The warm cheer of our holiday visit
froze once we saw you—
your spine, ribs, hips
prominent as winter tree limbs,
your eyes only holes
in a sunken head.

Ransacking the car for more food, I saw
our old neighbor, who'd found you,
folded in the front seat,
tears on his voice:
I'm sorry you had to see that.
He's lost over 300 pounds.

Driving away (and still today) I hate myself
for not finding you sooner, and resented
any horse with hay or shelter
or caregiver who cared.

Six years you'd stayed by us,
one year taken away,
and nearly your life.
The ice storm came two weeks later,
one day after your rescue.

Most of the year passed.
A kind couple came,
My God, what a beautiful horse—
We want him.

Your safety secure,
your future cantered into
my mind.

Roles reversed in the next life—
you his master,

not in pursuit of revenge
to abuse that beastly man,

but easily altering his apathy
with apples, a barn,
and a red plaid blanket.

Why else do we live?

For Chou

What I wanted to tell her
rests in the back pocket
of my heart.

It was just a small thing
to make her smile
and feel happy for the world.

I'd intended to tell her last week
but timing was off,
then she died.

I could tell any of you, but you might
not know how to handle it,
where to set it so
the light best shines through
to show its colorful fragments
of hope.

Our lovely little secret is safe
but sheltered,
forever unshared.

"and the other's gold"

Together, we'll visit our friend
who no longer knows us, and pluck
those pesky little whiskers
off her chin.

I'll keep the cat
you leave behind.

You'll come
when I call to say
the cancer's come back
or the diagnosis is dementia.

I'll go when you call
to say Joe just died.

We'll steady each other as we step
onto the bridge and say:
Stand tall, speak a little louder,
smile,
take my hand.

Something New

The kind neighbor's death at ninety
was Katie's first, at nine.

Nudged by her parents, Katie sat
at the kitchen table with his widow,
who mostly stared out the window
at the shed where he died.
She forgot to offer Katie a candy
from the blue bowl.

Katie mostly stared at the clock
and wished she knew
how long was long enough
for a nice visit.

She told about school
and her dog, then thought she
could count to ten
and say she must go,

but at ten she started over,
three times.
Finally she stood and said she had chores.

No honey, please don't go!
Her frightened tone frightened Katie.
No adult had spoken
to her this way.

But she touched her neighbor's shoulder:
Come over for a while. Mom will be home soon.
You can set the table, eat with us.
I'll walk you back home.

Her friend's eyes smiled
and relaxed.

No dear, I'll be fine,
you run along—just hurry back.

I hope one day when you're 88,
you'll know a girl who's
as good to you as you are to me.

Kate walked across the porch and waved.
The lowering sun returned
her reflection on the glass.

She wondered if she resembled that child
who might one day hear her say
those same words.

Small Comforts

(Reflections on 2009)

I

We dug Ozzie's grave in the north
flower bed a year before he died
softly of old age.
On the day before his last,
we squirted whipped cream
right in his mouth.
He was so happy.

I unwrapped the blanket to see his muzzle
before we tucked him into the earth, and covered him
with a clean white sheet of lime and a thick quilt
of good black dirt, in which I planted
nine jonquils—small ones, like him.

II

Some part of every tree broke. Every tree.
Trunks and great branches
crashing down throughout the night,
crushing our homes and any
hope that things might ever
be better—
smaller branches bending, snapping
apologetically, unable
to bear the weight of two days of ice,
and leaving no uncovered spot
big enough for the dog to go, when he had to.

The next day,
the trees surviving stood
like veterans or war orphans
in cruel, unsuitably lovely glitter,
their limbs oddly
bent, like compound
fractures.

The cashier would have stayed
in the warm store,
but he had dogs and chickens.
Each day, he made the round trip.
Sixty miles. I bought enough cans
of corn, coffee, and cat food
for a decade, to stop daily and
exchange our new greeting:
Got power yet?
On day nineteen, before I spoke,
he smiled.

III

> *On Sunday morning, moments after services had begun at Reformation Lutheran Church, Dr. Tiller, who was acting as an usher, was shot once with a handgun.*
> —The New York Times

In a silent moment
between prayer and song,
the shot that killed
was not, as she thought,

a hymnal dropped.
She was the second to him in the entry, but
there was nothing she, as doctor, could do.
Nothing but soothe his wife Jeanne
and wipe her face with a warm wet cloth and deliver,
later, fresh cinnamon rolls warmed.

IV

Late afternoon, late October—
I walked,
as I often do—
but not far,
before returning
for my white cotton sweater—
light, but just enough
across my shoulders
against the season's chill.

Elegy for Eight Words

The barricade arose on my dashboard
during the daily drive
with petit Gavroche shot
in the forty-fourth CD.

I left the battlefield of 1832 spinning,
my eyes dampened by Hugo's words:
The sound of the child hitting the pavement.

Heart pierced,
I crossed the hospital parking lot
to battle the work day.

Like a giant touching the earth,
Hugo distorted my orbit of ordinary—
Now

every door slammed,
every box dropped,
every heavy footfall,
and the child fell again.

Against propriety, I touched
a gentleman's face in our therapy room.
I stared in a baby's eyes
and briefly forgot where I was.

I adjusted the magnet holding Dave's youngest,
securing the photo to his locker,

and told him twice
on this day of great battle
that his boy is beautiful.

40° Out of 180—Song of the Scapula

Not even a fourth of possible. That's all
your arm and you will get without it—
forty degrees of forward.

Think of playing ball with the bat
held level with your belly.
Think of desperately knowing the answer
and waving your hand flush with your desk.
Think of combing the sides of your hair
only.
Think of cueing the cornets
with your baton not even
beyond the music stand.

But the scapula, like the wing of Gabriel,
glides along the ribs, its glenoid fossa
cradling the humeral head, coaxing it outward.
Then sublimely
the scapula swivels and bestows upon
the arm, the hand, the woman, the man
the wondrous gift of reach—out and up.

Up to dunk the ball
or whack it out of the park.
Up to toss tinsel on your Christmas tree.
Up to wave to your fella or your gal.

Up to comfort your child
or make a new one,

up to somersault,
up to dance hallelujah to your lord.

Be aware. Master the magic of the scapula!
Be guided by the angel's generosity:
out then up.

Reaching up before reaching out
restrains your range, pinches your potential.

Reach out. Then up,
and you might reach past
what you thought possible.

Ode to Estivation

I'd like to sing a song of summertime
and how it soothes my soul. Unfortunate
the fact that I detest this paradigm
of joy that melts me to a sweaty blot.

Despite long days, ice cream, bouquets soon gone—
attempts to cheer me up—I must escape:
a nap . . . a mere half hour . . . the slide beyond
is most agreeable so down I skate

into oblivion. Forget all chores,
responsibilities—the sofa calls.
Is it October yet? Response: my snores
while dreaming of our first and blessed snowfall.

Autumn shall come—till then, I whine and wait.
The wisest thing to do is estivate.

For My Young Friend Afraid He Learns Too Slowly

Your claim—
tallest in class
but dumbest—
slaps me back, hard.
Come spring, I'll show you
a secret:

The largest tree in our grove
of redbuds is always the last to bloom,
waiting as the welcome first color burst
of early spring fades and we think
maybe last year was its last.

Then it happens,
and its eruption of purple
glows more glorious
against the plain green leaves
of the smaller trees.

But it's November now.
The cold is back, cloaked in fall color,
and nothing about spring
seems that important.

Tutoring James

James wrote:

> *King was a great American.*
> *He helped white people*
> *mostly.*

I said:
> *Don't you mean King helped black people*
> *get the same rights*
> *as whites had?*

James said:

> *King showed the whites that blacks are good.*
> *Black folks already*
> *knew that.*

Slightly Up

The boy was already dead
when the firemen inhaled smoke
and broke down the door.
No ceremony, no medals,
but no less effort,
and no one said their names.

The gay young black Quaker,
called to Montgomery, told MLK:
*You know, that rifle in your pick-up window
and that pistol next to your keys
by the front door
don't look so good—
could we try another, less violent, way?*
Can you say his name?

Others refused to move to the back
before the chosen Rosa—
many bold and courageous,
risking lives and livelihoods—
their names conveniently erased.

In 1962, a calm naval captain
refused to launch the nuclear missile
to the American ship above
his submarine near Cuba, quietly preventing
World War III, so we could go along our little way
and never learn to say his Russian name.

Unnamed volunteers hid
in the bombed Murrah building ruins,

hoping discouraged rescue dogs could
find life and would keep trying,
as we, discouraged at times, try to encounter
Truth—even if trampled or forgotten—

and find that it arcs long, and bends
ever so slightly
Up.

Gym Friends

Ken doesn't care that my cat
hates the rain,
and I'll think no more
of his Ford's dented door,
and neither will dwell on Mel's pick
for best Asian hot sauce.

Yet our pretense of interest
has fashioned a web—
a safety net of care—
elasticized,
so we'll bounce
back to the gym

and each other.
S'racha.

The Domino Effect

The day after Dave died, I'd see someone
and say, *Look she's still alive,* surprised
as though that one death
were the first domino.

This setting up and falling has
played out since Adam,
and we suffer when the fallen domino
is from our own beloved box.

So many fall in October:
the cricket, the one-winged katydid,
the red geranium, the last tomato plant.
We ache that they are lovely, and leaving.

May calls out to comfort us;
we listen and want to trust
but linger in the loss, and wonder
if we should just head on down
and find our place in line.

Rose-Colored

We live as a rosebud too long—
enclosed, tight, straining the green girdle,
muzzling the petals' potential.

Finally we burst open,
full of achievement and accolades,
then think we will stay this way for eternity.

The mirror tells us otherwise,
or we slip and plant a nose in the garden gravel,
or the blossoms next to us on the stem
are pruned away.

It needn't be sad, this transformation,
but allows us an acceptable out
for those things we never
wanted to do anyway.

I'm sorry, I can't . . .
organize the bake sale,
edit your thesis,
adopt your dog,
run the fundraiser,
weed the church flower garden
go to the ball game or
(God forbid)
another high school graduation.
I'm sorry, I can't.

My petals are dropping.

Learning to Pray in French

My first try was *viens,*
come, be with me,
in the informal
conjugation.

As I came to know,
You are already
always
here.

I pruned my prayer to
Faire voir—show me,
Make me see—
as an apprentice asks
a master—respectfully,
yet hiding from my responsibility
to find You.

When I see You now
in the moon, in a mother's gaze,
in white tea towels
on the line, or in
a new poem or
an old hymn,
in a kitten's pounce, or
in the last marigold
before the frost,

then I pray
Viens voir—
Come, see what I found!
with the thrill of a child

et merci.

Cellar of the Heart

On dark days
we might
go to the cellar
to visit
our old pains—
harmless now
like dusty quarts
of green beans with
a good snake's skin
wrapped around, and
poke a few, offer a little guilt,
see if anything moves.

About the Author

LaDeana Mullinix is a native Kansan, now living in northwest Arkansas. She is a graduate of the University of Kansas and Texas Woman's University. She is a Quaker, a retired occupational therapist, a Master Gardener, and a Master Naturalist. She has written poetry since junior high but has only recently begun publishing her work.

www.ingramcontent.com/pod-product-compliance
Lightning Source LLC
Chambersburg PA
CBHW030915170426
43193CB00009BA/855